Snoopy and His Sopwith Camel

PRESENTING

The World War I flying ace ... here "giving his regards to old Broadway" before beginning another mission against his old arch enemy.

"Actually, World War I flying aces very seldom drank root beer," he explains.

But Snoopy was not like the others—"Doggondest daredevil I ever knew."
—The Red Baron

Snoopy and His Sopwith Camel

Charles M. Schulz

A FAWCETT CREST BOOK
Fawcett Publications, Inc. / Greenwich, Conn.

Part One

SNOOPY AND HIS SOPWITH CAMEL

THIS BOOK CONTAINS THE COMPLETE TEXT OF
THE ORIGINAL HARDCOVER EDITION.

A Fawcett Crest Book reprinted by arrangement with
Holt, Rinehart & Winston, Inc.

Library of Congress Catalog Card Number: 78-91065

Published by Fawcett World Library
67 West 44th Street, New York, N.Y. 10036
Printed in the United States of America

**Here's the World War I flying
ace being awakened to fly another
dawn patrol.**

"AT THREE O'CLOCK IN THE MORNING?!"

"Tell President Wilson to call me at ten."

**Here's the World War I flying ace
walking out onto the aerodrome
somewhere in France.**

I love my Sopwith Camel.

"Where's my stupid mechanic?"

"I hate it when he's late with my toasted English muffin."

Here's the World War I flying ace taking off on a dangerous mission ...our supply sergeant has told me to take good care of my Sopwith Camel.

Our supply sergeant hates me!

"Some people have dogs who chase cars, some people have dogs who bite the mailman, some people have dogs who dig up gardens...."

**Here's the World War I flying ace
back at the base... he is very
depressed... he is sitting alone in
a small French café drinking
root beer...**

**Actually, World War I flying aces
very seldom drank root beer...**

Ah! A shy country lass approaches...

I shall buy her a root beer and
impress her with my tales of
heroic deeds.

As the night goes on, we become
very friendly...

I think this simple country lass
has fallen for me...I could
probably become fond of her,
too, if she weren't so ugly!

The next morning I report to my commanding officer for orders... he is always impressed by my snappy salute!

**Word has it that the Red Baron
has been sighted near Toul...
my mission is to search him out,
and shoot him down.... I study
the map on the wall...**

Here's the World War I flying ace taking off again in his Sopwith Camel.

As I fly south following the Moselle River, I scan the skies for that familiar red Fokker Triplane.[1]

[1] As I recall, it was a shade between International Orange and Stearman Vermilion.

Too late! He has seen me first! A burst of tracers cuts across my wing!

This is what I get for sitting up all night drinking root beer.

Only my great skill as a pilot
enables me to return safely...my
ground crew is overjoyed to
see me.

The next day I am put on KP for
losing too many Sopwith Camels!
How humiliating!

Part Two

The war drags on.... News from
the front is all bad. A big enemy
push is expected at any moment.

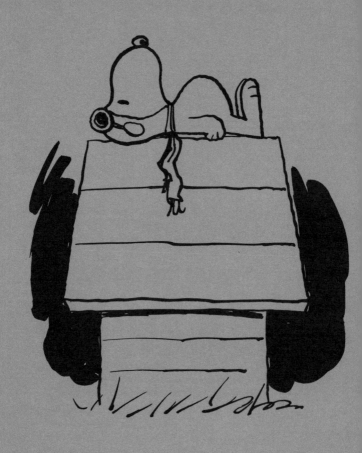

**It is difficult to sleep . . . one longs
for the comfortable beds of home.**

**Outside, flashes of artillery fire
can be seen in the distance...a
siren wails in the night...the
sky is dark...**[2]

[2] For more on dark skies, see my novel, IT WAS A DARK AND
STORMY NIGHT.

"What are we all doing here? This war is madness."

What's this? All pilots are
instructed to report to
headquarters immediately.

My first reaction is to realize that something is up.

We crowd into the briefing room.
The other pilots are inspired by
my quiet confidence.

This is the news we have been
waiting for. An ammunition train
is leaving Fère-en-Tardenois in
the morning. It will be well
guarded, but one lone plane flying
very low just might be able to get
through to it.

I, of course, immediately volunteer!

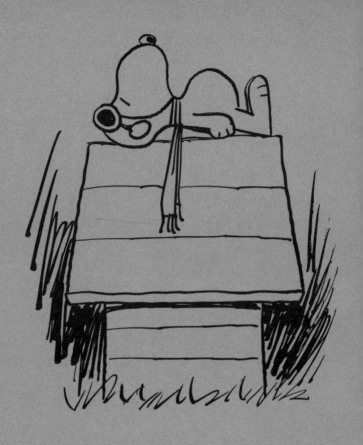

A few hours' rest before my
important mission... I wonder if
that shy country lass is thinking
of me....

When I awaken, the first faint
rays of dawn are beginning to
lighten the sky...it is cold...curse
this stupid war!

"Good morning, chaps...another important mission, eh what? But I daresay they are all important, eh what?"

**Here's the World War I flying ace
climbing into the cockpit of his
Sopwith Camel... I check the
instruments... they are all there...**

The ground crew bids me farewell.

"Switch off!" "Coupez!" "Contact?"
"Contact it is!"

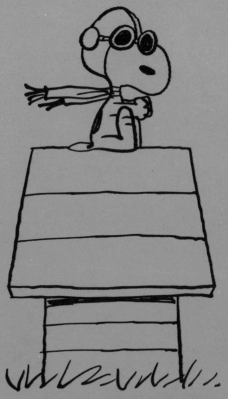

My route is along the Somme
valley... as the early morning sun
begins to warm the sky, I pass
Morlancourt Ridge not realizing
the dramatic role that this area is
someday to play.[3]

[3]See my next book.

As I fly over the trenches, I wave
to the poor blighters below....

**Blighters appreciate your
waving to them.**

"There it is! There's the ammunition train!"

As I wheel about, puffs of angry
flak appear in the sky.

And then another sound!
Machine-gun bullets tear through
the side of my Sopwith Camel...
it's the Red Baron!

Fighting the controls with every ounce of my strength, I manage to bring my stricken craft down behind enemy lines.

**I leap out of the burning cockpit,
and run for cover.**

I've got to find that ammunition
train, and destroy it.

**What's this? I can't believe it!
It's the shy country lass...she's
talking to the train engineer...
that girl is a spy!**

To think that I almost lost my
heart to her...I would have taken
her back to the states with me, if
she hadn't been so ugly.

I'll put on my famous disguise,
and find out their plans...

"Wo ist der root beer hall?"

Suddenly, I see my chance... I leap for the ammunition train, and destroy it.

A desperate bid for freedom!

**Here's the World War I flying ace,
back at the aerodrome somewhere
in France ... he thinks of the war,
the simple country lass who
deceived him, and the Red Baron ...
and he is plagued by the eternal
question....**

"Where's my toasted English muffin?"

The End